To Mary —
Love & all good wishes
Nicky

COMING UP TO MIDNIGHT

NICKY RICE

Coming Up to Midnight

London
ENITHARMON PRESS
1994

First published in 1994
by the Enitharmon Press
36 St George's Avenue
London N7 0HD

Distributed in Europe
by Password (Books) Ltd
23 New Mount Street
Manchester M4 4DE

Distributed in the USA
by Dufour Editions Inc.
PO Box 449, Chester Springs
Pennsylvania 19425

Text © Nicky Rice 1994
Cover image © Barry Flanagan 1994

ISBN 1 870612 48 5

The text of *Coming Up to Midnight* is set
in 10pt Ehrhardt by Bryan Williamson, Frome,
and printed by Antony Rowe Ltd, Chippenham

Acknowledgements

Some of the poems in this collection have previously appeared in *Ambit, Arts Council Anthology, Cumberland Review* (USA), *Encounter, The Green Book, London Magazine, New Poetry 4, The Observer, Outposts, Poetry Review, Prospice, South East Anthologies* 2 and 7, *South East Arts Review, Ver Poets Anthology, Writing Women, Yorick Books*. 'The Mirror' won 3rd prize in the Stroud International Poetry Competition 1978; 'Khephren – Fourth Dynasty' won 1st prize in the Outposts Poetry Competition 1978; 'Woodlice in a Hot Summer' won 3rd prize in the National Poetry Competition 1980; 'Devon Violets' won 4th prize in the National Poetry Competition 1984; 'Happy Ever After' won 2nd prize in the Outposts Poetry Competition 1985; 'Escape Route' won 1st prize in the St Albans Poetry Competition 1985; 'The Return' won 1st prize in the Outposts Poetry Competition 1987; 'Room Service' won 1st prize in the National Poetry Competition 1990.

The Enitharmon Press gratefully acknowledges the financial assistance of the University of Sussex (through the Ralph Lewis Award), and of the London Arts Board.

Barry Flanagan's linocut *Atlantic Moon*, published in 1983 by Waddington Graphics, is reproduced by kind permission of the artist. Enitharmon is indebted to Alan Cristea and Sarah Tooley of Waddington for the loan of the transparency.

for
Bobby
wherever she may be

Contents

I

Devon Violets *13*
Strawberries *14*
The Goodwife *15*
Penelope *16*
Happy Ever After *18*
Cinderella *20*
Brueghel: Peasant Wedding *21*
A Literary Exercise *22*
Nature Study *23*
Counting the Rows *25*
The Mirror *26*
Dreams *27*
Escape Route *28*

II

A Winter's Tale *31*
A Walk in Winter *32*
New Year *33*
Persephone *34*
Rocks *35*
Wild Geese *36*
Tortoise *37*
Worms *38*
Woodlice in a Hot Summer *39*
On the Railway Bridge *40*
The Return *41*
Proteus *42*
Adam *43*

III

Ground Rent *47*
Fuchsias at Coum Duv *49*
Going North *50*
Lindisfarne Priory *51*
Lament for Wilderness *52*
Sound and Light *53*
Khephren – Fourth Dynasty *55*
In Search of Homer *56*
At Pompeii *57*

IV
Transplant *61*
Waiting *62*
The Ailing Aunts *63*
Geriatric Ward *64*
Room Service *65*
The Funeral *66*
Lazarus Rising *67*
Mother's Room *68*

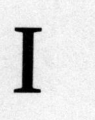

I

Devon Violets

The maids always had some in their bedroom
with the hair-tidy and jars of vanishing cream.
I knew it wasn't quite out of the top drawer;
my sophisticated aunt from London used Soir de Paris.

Grandmother used it, but then she hadn't much experience.
Her daughters were rather ashamed of her. It smells
like a brothel in here, they used to say, and
sprinkled her with lavender water when we went out.

In the West Country you could buy it everywhere.
Fat ladies on charabanc trips carried it home
to dressing-tables in Birmingham, with pieces of pottery
marked 'Clovelly' and memories of clotted cream.

Years later I came across it again, having quite
forgotten in the eventful meantime. By then I had
learned the bite behind certain platitudes, a broken
heart, for instance, and life's not all honey.

We were on holiday again, but the children
were mine this time and not a father between them.
They were in love with summer, the austere
tors of Dartmoor, farmhouses and buttermilk

and giddy insects shrilling under the trees.
They knew I cried sometimes at night, but the
Souvenir Shop could cope with most contingencies.
The bottle was just the same, dumpy, inelegant,

the same scribble of mauve flowers on the label
by some rather inferior draughtsman. I didn't want
to smell it, but of course I had to. When I smiled
my mouth felt like broken glass.

That night I threw it into the darkness with
Grandmother's bones and the thin spectres of the
maids with their stockings and spilled
face powder, and when we got home

I noisily ransacked all the cases and said
I must have left it in the bedroom at Ilfracombe.

Strawberries

He brought me strawberries,
arriving hot, disordered, in grey flannel
on a summer afternoon. Bewildered by my grief
he'd pilfered coppers in the changing-room,
alone with the expressionless white tiles,
sweat loading the air like incense,
the rifled garments menacing with empty limbs
longer than his eight years.

He brought me strawberries
clutching his punnet like the Grail,
my favour at his heart where the
crushed fruit bled onto his shirt front;
and behind the freckles, the babyish
blunt features, his concern on tiptoe, breathlessly
imploring my delight.

He brought me strawberries
remembering his other summers,
the blistering sweetness on his tongue,
the blue uncomplicated days, his mother
smiling. It was Elysium he brought
with strawberries carefully, in cupped hands.

But the juice was draining out of them so fast
he could not save it, and I watched the years
leak from his fingers and his hands were wet
with them and my face was wet with tears.

And he looked at me and knew what he had lost.

The Goodwife

She never really made it,
a thin nervous woman but
ineffective.
Education docked abruptly
by an early marriage, years
of commitment to late night
shopping and the cheaper
cuts of meat, it was
a lifetime of missed concerts,
galleries unvisited, libraries
at the wrong end of town.
Even sex was almost a closed
book in spite of several
children whom she wore as
shields against too close
acquaintance with herself.

We coincided sometimes over
coffee cups, her history
passing between us, thinly
sliced. Then I moved away
but still picture her
nervous behind the china
with her empty hands, waiting
for heaven to fill them
yet aware habit dies hard
and probably she'll reach
even the gates of Paradise on
early closing day.

Penelope

This year
she wears a one-piece swimming costume, leaving
bikinis

to the young
who have no hang-ups and whose skin fits them
so beautifully

while hers,
she thinks, resembles seaweed, shrivelling,
desiccated

in white sand
where the blue tideless Aegean nibbles
the shore.

Mountains
this morning wear the sky at a modish angle
and watching them

she remembers
seasoned Ulysses, island-hopping towards Ithaca,
dislikes her husband,

recumbent, boiled
in socks and city lace-ups because sandals
hurt his feet,

but acquiesces
when he straddles her, bearing sun-tan lotion
like a votive urn,

anointing
her parched flesh, his hands lubricious, his face
shadowed

against the racked joints
of the olive trees, the cypresses' dark spires
and suddenly

it is Ulysses
mounting her on the cracked earth where ants scurry,
the beetle hefts its wings'

dead weight
and fragile, papery, the poppy opens its veins
among the corn.

The ferries
are putting out now from the shore, the suitors
with Walkmans

have departed
to water-side tabernas. Presently she will
return

with him
to the self-catering arrangements where the wardrobe
is not large enough

for two
and the plumbing is capricious, in the cramped house
that is not Ithaca.

Happy Ever After

Mostly they were princesses though they did
the usual girlish things, letting men climb up
their long hair or taking a toad to bed.

Their dates are only approximate, circa
once-upon-a-time. Conditions were feudal and
architecture aspired to castles with pointed turrets.

Their mothers usually died in childbed
and fairies attended their christening, handing out
gifts or curses, depending on their mood.

They were lonely children, their confidantes
old cobwebby crones at spinning-wheels in forgotten rooms
or hunchbacks with a chip on their shoulder

or decapitated horses. Fathers were well-meaning
but weak, and often promised them to monsters
for political reasons, or grew randy in middle age,

bringing home a new bride still young enough
to resent competition. For they were all beautiful,
snow white or rose red, nothing mousy

or middle of the road about them. They were
chaste, industrious, docile and thick. Anyone
less gullible would have slept elsewhere when she

discovered the lumpy mattress and would certainly
have closed the door on the plausible old lady
with the poisoned apples. But they never questioned

what fate had to offer, allowing themselves to be
locked in towers for a hundred years or dressed in rags
and abandoned to the wild and still they remained

extravagantly romantic, befriending grizzly bears
and spending the best years of their lives making shirts
for wild swans. They knew the end of the story you see,

the grand denouement when the chrysalis would rupture
and the prince step from its tatters radiant, with his
redeeming kiss. In our dark towers we sit alone,

watching the light fade and the forest creeping closer.
The shining armour hangs from a nail in the wall now
and the glass slipper shattered years ago.

Cinderella

Thirty years on and visits the chiropodist
weekly. The Prince jogs night and morning,
wearing trainers and bouncing annoyingly
on the balls of his feet, which she construes
as a sly dig at her incipient bunion.
What has he got to be so smug about?

She knows her feet are no longer pretty
but whose fault was that, cramming them
day after day into those ridiculous slippers
until they simply splintered under her?
What is he, some kind of foot fetishist?
And so incurably romantic! Nothing suits her,

he says, so well as the rags she was wearing
when they dragged her in from the kitchen.
He'd have her back there again, given half
a chance, in a rundown cottage at the back of
beyond, with no washing machine and a coal range.
He likes open fires. Cinders turn him on.

Her sisters settled for spinsterhood in the end;
they wear orthopaedic shoes and value their freedom.
Sometimes she thinks they came off best.
And yet – she remembers the ball, the flowers
and wine, the music. How the chandeliers
glittered, crystal and gold! How she admired

her reflection dancing in his eyes, his arms
around her, her skirts a frou-frou of silk,
organza, chiffon, the toes' darting quicksilver,
the taut glass arch of the instep
whirling through polka, cotillion, schottische –
the little, little feet!

Oh, Fairy Godmother, with your magic wand,
touch these cold embers. Make things
right again. The pumpkin is ready,
the mice agog behind the skirting – but hurry!
The hands are coming up to midnight.

Brueghel: Peasant Wedding

It is a stage set for a pantomime,
the peasants in their comic clothes
and Christmas cracker hats, thick calves
in coloured stockings and broad, slabby feet

tramping across the canvas where the
giant victuallers steal the limelight;
players tenderly cuddling their bagpipes
like contented stomachs

while the vintner, in his sober suit,
carefully replenishes flagons, the child
beside him, stupid with gluttony,
engulfing food and fingers indiscriminately.

It is all trestles and trenchermen,
corn-gold and scarlet as apples
like a harvest festival.
And indeed the hanging sheaves,

accomplished fact of harvest,
dwarf the bridal crown
and the table's bold diagonal
asserts priorities,

returning the bride to her background,
her bread and butter world where parents,
relatives, still hedge her in
the thickets of childhood.

In this red-blooded revelry she has no place.
Under the tipsy crown she sits, eyes closed,
remembering her shining hour,
in such abundance knowing nothing of

the spent barns of winter,
the unexpected famine.

A Literary Exercise

Later she decided that he was the worst poem
she ever wrote, displaying all the shortcomings
of inexperience and a few besides. At the time
she thought him magnificent, couldn't get enough

of him. She hadn't learned the value of revision
yet, the importance of taking a second look.
It was all too one-sided. She'd had the words for years
in her bottom drawer and simply crammed him

into them, cutting a few corners on the way. There
was plenty of hackneyed imagery to hand and plenty
of role models too, killing dragons, breaking spells,
outwitting wicked queens and hacking their way

through thickets into the land of Happy Ever After,
so he was all Grail and Galahad, clear-eyed, blond,
every girl's knight in shining armour. He was
so ham, so utterly predictable. He was so damn sweet.

Of course, like all unsuccessful composition,
he was written at night when lamp light was
sympathetic and she was hyped on rhetoric
and too much wine. Over breakfast, rain at the

window and smears of marmalade between them, he
didn't look so good. She should have finished
it then, but she hung on, hoping for a punch-line
that would justify all the platitude, but at last

she had to acknowledge that reality demands an idiom
altogether harsher. That was when she added
the final stanza. She put him away at the back
of a drawer with other discarded MSS and nowadays

she wonders at times if someone else has made
a better job of him, even recites him
occasionally to very close acquaintances.
She can still remember every line.

Nature Study

Sheets bluster on the line, and nylon underwear
rounded provocatively with air. It is the
first drying day since Autumn. One daffodil
has survived the weather's excavations, but
I think the ceanothus tree is dead.
In Manchester you tell me there is still snow

in high places and the pervasive north-western rain
mourns at your window. O, that north-western rain!
I used to peer through it looking for the south
and the sun and a spring tide that never came.
And I used to do the washing every day as you do
in the new kitchen with the red formica. Outside

were vegetables and your swing and upstairs
there was always a baby crying as our numbers grew.
In doorways the mats were sopping.
'One day,' I used to tell myself, 'over the next
hill...,' believing like you that everything
in some gardens is lovely and the road would

take us there, arriving in Spring with a flush
of cherry blossom and the first hint of a heatwave.
But roads continue. We have travelled over
many hills and still a late frost surprises us
and Winter's savage landscaping rearranges
the future in a pattern we had not bargained for.

The garden is always beyond us. Perhaps that is why
we planted Adam and Eve in one, grew them there
naturally like the flowers, until the angel
banished them, like you, to Manchester
with the wet roofs and the hopeless washing.
Yet each year they sowed and planted. What else

could they do in the long Spring days
with the wind blowing over the empty borders
and mouths to feed at home, counting the cost,
working the unsympathetic clay as you do
among your no-nonsense cabbages, mud on
your shoes? Could Paradise still seem

a possibility? The question hangs in
mid-air like the yellow lamp of the daffodil
sagging already on its tall stalk.
Rain and wind move inwards from the sea
bringing no satisfactory answer.
The trees cross themselves continually.

Counting the Rows

Mummy, did you knit me, you asked at six,
watching me grapple with an awkward pattern,
but that was many years ago and many patterns.
I still knit; the wool is sympathetic. It fills
the empty space between my hands and mends
the edges of my days while I await your letters,
keeps winter out.

And now it seems you are a knitter also
but your design is global, a weave of trade
routes and spice islands, of ancient causeways,
river valleys, mountain tracks, and when you telephone,
your voice, a strand drawn thin, runs up
and down volcanoes, winds and unwinds
through jungles,

threading the miles across hot continents.
Hall – hallo. Are you all right? Yes, I'm
all right. Are you? Sometimes the strand pulls
thin and we can scarcely hear each other.
On the Equator, you tell me, nights can be
treacherous. You will need warm clothing – wool
next to the skin,

but your yarn is unfamiliar, the instructions
written in a language I cannot understand. Must I
unravel last year's fabric, take up another thread?
My knitting is therapeutic. If yours could be
so simple, subdued to the comfortable shuttle of
purl and plain, the certainty of knowing the wrong
side from the right –

but not this frantic tapestry that hurts the eyes,
this haphazard geometry of stops and starts
and new directions! Mummy, did you knit me?
Well, if I did, nobody warned me how many years
this work would hang so heavy from my needles,
nothing prepared me for the finished article when
I cast you on.

The Mirror

She was all right in her natural habitat,
lurking in lakes, endlessly redefining herself in rainpools,
but I carried her home like a trophy to hang on the wall,
tried to domesticate her, get her to fall in with my view,

but she wouldn't. Oh, she pretended of course
to have no mind of her own, copied my poses and gestures
and was always glad to see me, but there was a hint of parody in it
and I didn't see how she looked when my back was turned.

She seemed to come to life when people were there
(Bishop Berkeley would have loved her)
and nothing escaped her huge, Cyclopic eye. At first it was
like living with God or a large silver conscience

but then I discovered at heart she was just a cheap voyeuse.
She had a memory long as injured pride and her
big bulby blur hid a maw like an ocean. She was greedy.
Alice went at one gulp, but that was a long time ago.

She's wiser now and nibbles insidiously,
a smile or a dimple here, a jaw-line there.
So for ages I wasn't aware that she was short-changing me
but then my failings began to ache like amputations

and people stopped noticing me, so I knew something
was wrong. She was damaging my image.
One of these days I'll disappear completely
unless I shatter her illusions.

But she'll give as good as she gets, besides she's cunning,
she'll only divide and divide, disgorging her replicas,
the stumps and candle-ends of history.
She could people a planet with dead selves.

So I'll lose her instead but I'll do it at night. She's powerless then
and needs light to function by like a lop-sided vampire.
I'll abandon her on a cold mountainside and there she can lie
in the grass all day, doing no harm and mimicking the sky.

Dreams

I think of them as thin,
almost two-dimensional, a pack of cards
dealing themselves in a mad game with no rules
and they hold all the aces.
It's sheer chance. No way of telling

which one will show its face.
Sometimes the certainty of homecoming,
the kisses, the made fortune.
Or the disgrace, the nakedness in the market-place,
the gold coins that dissolve in daylight.

It's the joker you have to watch.
He's a sly fox. He'll smile
into your eyes and then suddenly undo the catch,
letting out the casualties,
the maimed with their terrible amputations.

And they all cheat quite shamelessly,
shuffling memories, getting the addition wrong.
The sea successfully covers its dead. The heather
blows on the headland, safe anchorage in sight.
Then you awaken and it is grey, grey.

One day they may detach themselves, float up into daylight.
Strange to meet one at noon and not know the difference.
But at least I'll sleep well,
my mind a no man's land,
a bony theatre full of darkness.

Escape Route

I boarded this train late, night coming down
and the station thorny with tenterhooks,
the megaphone announcing departures, its mouth
gaping, aghast at what it is saying.

The route is unfamiliar, but they all thread
the dark forest, pick up the dropped crumbs.
Wheels going round in circles, reiterate, reiterate
an impossible argument, the miles torn off,

jettisoned behind us and the lopped track
whining. People make room for me, move
baggage and heavy overcoats, their faces
like occupied countries, colourless, shuttered,

their cases crammed with lifetimes folded
between layers of newspaper. They have
pulled my horizon closer, hooding the glimmer
of infinity. I shall not stride into it now,

the wind's throttle, the wildfire of stars,
but shuffle with these travellers, blinkered
and unamazed towards a terminus that repeats the past.
So, while the steel clatters to conclusion

and the hours unreel, night shapes
crowding the window and falling away like pain,
let me forget the dying distances,
let me not think of them again.

II

A Winter's Tale

A tale for winter, brief as winter's light.
Chestnuts and chapped fingers scorch at the hearth
while Grandmother's thick gutturals
people the room with demons.

Branches clutch at a pewter sky. The lake
has wrapped their reflection in a membrane of ice
and a harsh north-easter drives the hunter home,
his satchel fat with Christmas.

Snow has redeemed the blood among the fir trees
but the owl's scream menaces the dusk
and children, cold with delicious terror,
dawdle on the stairs to bed

where Grandmother's hobgoblins tease their dreams,
her sheeted legends keening through their sleep
howl down the predator's descent,
the whimper in the forest.

A Walk in Winter

The snow records my journey,
opening dark foot-holes behind me,
crusting each rut and cranny
in the road ahead.
Above, branches suffer their white hairs
with dignity, like old age.

I am content in this stopped season.
It is not that summer is unbeautiful,
merely that my weather matches with January,
ends and not beginnings are my country.
Here the lean backbone of winter
gives nothing, asks nothing in return.

Feeling is locked in ice. Memory stiffens
to the narrow vista of the Christmas card.
These are the acres of the snowman
flattening himself into his background,
only the bearded muffler, the sugar-frosted hat
between him and obliteration.

Sudden light combs the dull sky.
Water rouses itself in pond and ditch,
begins to shake off winter. Somewhere
far down roots are about their business.
The year is on the move again, but I
am stalled in a white hush below the ice-cap.

New Year

The interruption of Christmas
is behind us now.
We have folded up the festivities

and the ravaged tree
battles with January
in a corner of the garden.

This is the dead of the year,
the small hours
when the pulse falters

and infirmity goes to the wall.
Beyond the window
a wild country is growing

where a thin sunset lights
tinder of field and sky.
We should hold funerals now,

commit last year's distemper
to a spectacular incineration
while the carping wind

rises to a scold's shriek
and trees stand close, branches bent
like the fingers of arthritics,

but knitting, knitting,
abominable tricoteuses
attending the death-stroke.

Already the new year sinks its claws
into our resolution.
We shall carry these scars a twelvemonth.

Persephone

The flowering cherry effervesces
over its tall stem.
Primulas button the soil's homespun,

even the rose trees
open at the seams, reclaiming inches
lost to the pruning knife.

Far from their roots now
they have quite forgotten the long uphill struggle
and ask little

to hallow their seasonal mysteries,
some sunlight, the bees' good offices,
nothing at all from me,

tall gangling vegetable
suddenly amongst them without benefit
of leaf, frond or flower.

At my door the north wind grinds its iron,
the cutlery of winter.
Promontories of ice harden around me.

Is there no way upwards
to the sun?
The earth is more hospitable,

keeping open house
in the sealed chambers of the subsoil,
damp circuit of the beetle and the worm.

Down there no one is turned away.
The small fry of the bedrock
get such scantlings as they can

and will unhusk my grist like buried treasure.
Stone and fibre will rub shoulders with me
and the pleached root take me in.

Rocks

That day they were not white horses but mammoths
that thundered on the shore. The wind,
wearing your yellow dress, beckoned us
frantically as we lurched and slid
through stony bric-à-brac,
the harsh hard core of the sea bed.

All day the breakers had it in for us
and now scuttled us suddenly, among rocks.
Skeletons in the sea's closet, these,
a fist of knuckles bunched under the tide
they'd crush a hull to eggshell,
run a granite forefinger clean through timber
to fetch up in the creaking fo'c'sle and tip
a score of mariners into the waves' trawl.

Now in these isolate waters pickings are sparse.
Nursing their grievances they crouch
like starveling predators, agog to snap
such crusts of negligible traffic
the careless sea might toss in their direction.
All year I bore their teeth marks. You
left a ribbon of skin six inches long,
meshed for a while in the kelp
about their stumps, to swill up later
with the shuttling tide and flap and rot
in the salt garbage at the sea's edge.

Wild Geese

This dusk is autumnal, early, cold,
barred door and blinded window keeping
the weather out and none but I abroad
and the small tenantry of ditch and field,

about their business in rank tunnels sunk
by August rain. The morning's storm sky
is scoured clean, like a mind made up and
evening slips through my fingers, its black bolts

swathing the colours of daylight and the house
hunched monolithic at my back. No sound but
the sough of leaves where a gust tousles
the rags of summer.

But suddenly air thickens under the
rafters of the sky, throbs to the pulse
of their advance, the high-strung
horizons strident with their clamour.

The steady creak of wings, their bodies'
clots of darkness on the dark following,
while the stretched frantic necks
lie on the wind of their migration.

They are like summer departing, departing
and I recall the child, face pressed
to the window, while summer visitors
recede, calling goodbye, with their

luggage of souvenirs and sunlight.
Will they arrive, these hopeful travellers,
set up their paradise elsewhere, far
from these bleak acres I inherit?

It is done. No dint or scar on the
bared distances records their passage
and the familiar emptiness moves in,
the hollow corridors opening on nothing.

Well, it is the season of farewells.
The nights grow colder.

Tortoise

A blunt head prodding air, loose pleating
at the neck like the folds of an old man's
muffler, jaw opening thin as a scissor cut
and the unamazed slate eyes. The
intractability of that rigid waistcoat

against the soft belly, the vitals!
What keeps him in there, bonding flesh
to carapace? If he could take it off,
discard it for a while like some old roué
uncorsetting, the limbs flexing, ecstatic!

I found an empty shell beside a ditch,
an ornamental box that wind and rain had polished
to a gloss. This was no comic interlude –
the rind scraped clean, the kernel prised
from its housing. Whatever did this meant business.

The bargain hunters were in already. A knot
of legs and antennae like red wires
seethed in one corner, trying it for size.
In nature's thrift shop nothing is wasted –
shells, leavings. Dead men's shoes.

Worms

Tube-shaped, but pliable. Sometimes as much
as thirty metres from the head end to the tail
and thick with it,

the glistening skin packed tight, for they'll eat
all before them – garbage, dregs – some invade
living tissue,

clamp themselves to the gut and wring it dry. All
see eye to eye with corpses. Death is a way of life
to them

and they make efficient undertakers, disposing
of the soft parts, the appendages, with a minimum
of fuss.

All's grist to them but soil's their staple. They
cram themselves neck and crop, leaching the nutrients,
the good salts,

and afterwards void small replicas of themselves,
cast from the mould of their own casing.
It's said

if you cut a worm in two, both halves will survive.
Once, as a child, I chopped clean through one
and found it

full of progeny, shelled them like pease, but
the cut ends never moved. And sometimes the cat
leaves me

one on the doorstep, quite limp and ragged
where her claws punctured the tender membrane.
Such pain

is voiceless. Like lizards, fish, they have
no vocal cords and they die quietly, making
no bones about it.

Woodlice in a Hot Summer

By day they keep their distance.
Only a susurration in the leaves reveals them,
like a wringing of dry hands,
or a casualty from time to time,
a small spoonful of legs, pedalling helplessly
to shrivel on the concrete.

They are so dry. No moisture anywhere
to ease the friction of those scaly plates
about the carcase, down there among
the parched thistles, the crazed pieces of broken pot.
Water is all. I guard my cisterns while the garden hums
keeping its own counsel, but the wind betrays me,
shedding its cool odours on the grass,
broadcasting my reservoirs. The nights are hazardous.

In the dank lee of wall or doorstep
they cluster motionless and menace
by sheer weight of numbers,
or scuttle from the nucleus at a wicked speed.
Once an unwary guest went out there barefoot;
under his soles they were busy and harsh as shingle.

Summer advances and the sun
mimics its old fury
when mammoths trod the endless burning steppe
and trumpeted their famine.
Millennia dissolve. Under the tiny carapace
memory thunders in the blood.
Over sill and doorpost they swarm,
remembering the rain forest.

On the Railway Bridge

Around and underneath us steel girders
creak and fret, a long-winded reproach
that jars to the touch like electricity.

We man the bridge together; captain
and mate, we strut and swagger,
pull levers of air

and semaphore instructions into space
while the wind scalps us.
From this perspective, November roosts

in branches sharp as bristles, slate roofs
tackle the hill, gardens and yards unfence,
houses expose themselves, curtains that sag

at steamy windows, disconsolate washing,
ladders, dustbins, bicycles. Figures dwindle
to pin men, extravagantly angled at knee and elbow,

that move like hinges until distance rubs them out.
Along the track, between wet nettles
and the dripping elders, silence assembles.

The air pressed to our faces like wet linen
starts to unfix the afternoon's thin colours
and house lights have drawn a street map,

but down there no train arrives.
The cutting is a hollow only, a receptacle.
Darkness enters the mould.

The Return

Must it be always thus, a hard
homecoming among rocks grey like pumice,
the wind endlessly scouring its hearth stone
and the hills' lean line?

No surplus, no profligate kisses here.
The door slams shut in summer's face.
Let her breathe her last elsewhere,
knee-deep in dead flowers. Here

is a land with empty pockets,
a harsh economy of wind and rock,
a landscape honed everywhere to
a fine edge, the jagged promontories,

the lance of the rain. Even
the curlew sharpens his cry
as he wheels and climbs
into cold weather.

And the loneliness! The last byre
five miles back, the door lamenting
on its split hinge, the stalls empty.
You could search all day for a fatted calf

in these iron hills.
There is no pity in them.

Proteus

I am water

and absolute, keeping
myself to myself.
When the rest crawled landwards, I remained
and watched their painful progress to the shore,
the ache of severed roots,
abrasion of inhospitable rock
where the cliffs open like incisions
and the cut walls laid back
offer themselves to the wind's scalpel.

My element is here
with the carnage of the ocean floor
where fish eats fish, but time
gnaws its own tail.
The wash of history laps at my wake
turns with the shuttling tide
and present, past and future
open like a shell.

Ask me no questions, landsman,
(not for your eyes will I unpick the years
crusted like barnacles about your hull)
nor seek to net me in
the tattered meshes of your purpose.
I am the source, the whirlpool,
the elemental trough where life
broke from the darkness.

I am water.

Adam

Only the darkness turning upon itself
endlessly, in a small circle.
Then suddenly upheaval like a confluence of oceans,
the slap of atom upon atom,
the elements encountering like granite
headlong, pulling form out of diffusion,
and the mind coming in, like a spring tide,
and they knew themselves, Adam
and the universe together.

Curled like a foetus in the astonished grass
while his heart measured the moments in his ears
and the greedy bags of his lungs filled up,
what answer could he make to the morning
opening around him, raucous and bright with being,
or the shadows in the orchard at the day's decline
catching him unawares between the trees?
What was he like, this template, in the time before the apple
and his first sly nibble of divinity?
Did he really jerk to the puppet-master's twitch
with painted acquiescence on his face
and glassy indifferent eyes?

Or was the germ already knocking in his skull,
fecund with foreknowledge and a vision
that could trample fences of space and time
and go leapfrogging with infinity?
And did he know also that he hung upon the lip
of humanity's unuttered scream and fathered
the bloody footsteps faltering to Calvary?
And if he did know – brave Adam!
walking forward, shouldering centuries.

III

III

Ground Rent

We had to climb up from the village
in the heat. A mile to the top it was
between hedges bossed with small hard
strawberries, black underneath at noon when

there was no shadow. Then the hedges gave out.
The sign said 'To the Moor', pointing eastwards,
but it could have been any direction, the moor
was all about us. The village sat in its lap.

The place barely tolerated us. I could feel resentment
in the dust spilling itself on our shoes, briar
guarding the path, the heather dark as a frown
as if the moor said, 'You may come this far,

no further,' remembered farmers' words at dusk,
'If you scratch her back she'll pick your pocket,'
and stories of rash Jack Endacott
who laughed at the warning, built his hut

in her very back yard and swore
he'd wring a crop from her stringy flanks,
slept sound at night though the moor
was breathing down his neck.

But she was a comfortless bedfellow, mattressed
on grit, tight-fisted, dry as a stick.
The harrow twisted on her skeleton acres,
snapped in her flinty spine. Thistle

and scrub were all he could gather in
and lichenous rock of a darker fathering.
When the money was gone she wouldn't leave him,
followed him back to the empty barn

and the stripped house, sat down on the doorstep
waiting, while nettles and thorn
inched closer, grass had a foot in the door,
creeper prised at the windows

and climbed to the eaves. Under the floor
roots got a purchase, lengthened. The moor
does nothing by halves
and owns the freehold, allowed no grace,

in her own season called in the lease.

Fuchsias at Coum Duv

But you did not say there would be fuchsias.
Yarrow you said and I found it, cloth of gold
yellower than the flat amber of the eyes of sheep.

Gorse you said, thistles and heather –
everywhere heather fighting for foothold
in that starved stony kingdom

and everywhere faltering to a standstill
in faceted grey rock, where the hill
shows its bones.

And the lake was there where God had set it down,
curved still from the cup of his hand,
its dark skin ruckled to the harrow of the wind.

Mountains encircled us, like the profile
of dead kings on catafalques, forehead and sunken chin
cutting the shadows while the dusk advanced.

I thought of oaks and omens,
barrows and standing stones while we returned
along the rutted alley,

sheep-droppings underfoot, grass to the ankles,
brambles unwilling to release their hold;
and overhead the unexpected fuchsias

dipped and bowed, a tangled scarlet smear,
as if some hunter of the dark
hurried ahead of us on bloodied feet.

Going North

Cullercoats – Silloth – Morebattle –
sign-posts carry words that seem to threaten
as if scrawled there to warn marauders off,
now merely quaint, amusing – something
to interrupt the drab recitatif of coach
itineraries, egg the imagination on.
Plenmeller could be an instrument
for putting stones in horses' hooves.
Throckley sounds like a cleaning agent.
But places? Somewhere to go to, be at, live?
They seem implausible, impossible.

Do people send letters post-marked Humshaugh?
buy groceries at Chimside, have nervous breakdowns
at Kirkwhelpington? Are there family rows
on Sundays between Low Church and high water
at Seaton Sluice? Do they lay cinder paths around
stone cottages in Thrunton, with sheep's bones
at the bottom of the garden in a landscape
signed by Turner, raise cabbages at High Force
in an endless argument with nature,
never waste words at Haltwhistle, or mince
matters or laugh when the wind is in the east?

Do they get married, join the library, make tea
at Snitter and Shilbottle and Pity Me?

Lindisfarne Priory

Night Stairs to Dormitory, says the legend
on the wall, but who ascended here?
On what nocturnal business? And why?

The havoc of this place discloses nothing
but the way the weather has taken it apart,
uncoupled wall and buttress – sills almost
gone under,

the west front intact still but flimsy,
like stage furniture, pierced with a window-
aperture high up, an arch that opens into space –

and the wind that is always blowing here,
its hoot and wail across the dunes,
the throes of grass and thistle beaten
flat,

and the sea idling beyond the salt marsh
until the tide returns, drowning the causeway
to the mainland when the island rides adrift.

Rock, wind and water write their own record.
No autograph recalls a figure on the narrow
steps – small-statured, tonsured, corded,
cowled

against the chill leaking from stone and stone.
No, nor the absolute faith of the man
through how many dark nights treading

this ground that would absorb him, reading
the repetition of seasons, tides – his certainty
of order and appointed time and God's high water
building,

awaiting the breakers, the tumult on the shore,
blind to the silence stretching beyond,
the tideless ocean that affords no mooring.

Lament for Wilderness

Panting excursion coaches regurgitate
a cud of pak-a-macs and camera cases.
Toilets, the signs tell us, Town Centre,
Information Office, Give Way to Traffic
from the Right. We take the turning labelled Sea.

But surely this was where – remember? – the trees
wouldn't capitulate but struggled on almost to
the water's edge. Remember that holiday in August?
Beyond the sand was open sky and grassland – no town
at all. Remember high tide and the gulls coming in

on the heel of the weather? Later there was tea
in a garden somewhere with cream that dawdled
from the spoon and the wasps sang and staggered –
jam-drunk and stupid with the dying season.
Where does the past go when we have finished with it?

Thin rain begins. The shelters on the promenade
mop up the overflow from fish and chip bar, steak-house.
It is the hour of the packed lunch, the sandwiches
(vacuum-wrapped), the tepid Thermos. We find
a pub, hoping for rafters, chimney-corners,

but the décor is brash, the barmaid bored, the food
uncompromising. Homeward eventually, turning
inland from the bay, I scan the barbered coastline,
searching for roots, for something native growing,
but when – next month, next year – I say to you

remember that day in August? we shall think of
concrete, plastic, glass – thin bloodless materials,
haphazardly assembled, ineptly grafted, that suffocate
the ancient stock. What of the gulls then, the empty
wide sand? Is this the end of them,

annulled because unremembered? Or does the grass
still move under the wind's hand, the wasps' whine
nagging the heat and silence, where the past goes
when we have finished with it,
when it has finished with us?

Sound and Light

Enthralled spectators at the sound and light, we
slap mosquito bites, sipping the overpriced thin beer from
tepid glasses. The lamps flash on and off, flash on
and off. Statistics rain like bullets from the microphones.

'The Great Pyramid has a base area larger than the combined
extent of five cathedrals.' (But in the Ascending
Corridor we had to walk bent double and the trapped air
stank. No room for a sarcophagus to pass.)

'Upwards of two million blocks of stone were used
in its construction.' (They had to haul the coffin
up and lower it into the Burial Chamber – the final
block slotted into position under the capstone.)

'Life on this plateau has not changed significantly in
five thousand years.' (The camels rock and strut on match-
stick legs, the Sphinx studies the sand. Dark-faced hawkers
pestered us with tacky leather goods and beads and

plastic amulets when we emerged in the white glare
at noon, blinded with heat and history.)
'Man fears time, but time fears the pyramids,' the voices drone
and all around the past asserts the dominance of stone,

for these were built to last. Have lasted. The
pyramids we built were not so durable, soft at the core,
and when they crumbled there was no sound and very little
light, so there was nothing for it but to cross

the barren land to Giza where the river, carrying
Egypt on its back, heads for the delta and we meet
the pyramids on their own terms, uncompromising, stark,
pitched against the sun and sand in ghastly clarity.

(O Mother Isis, let me not walk upside-down in darkness.
Guard me from Set and deserts and water me in the dry months
when the river sinks. Remember the book that I must carry with me
and under the bandages lay the scarab beetle on my heart.)

The voices cease. The lights are setting one by one.
Cheops, Khephren, Mykerinos follow each other into the west.
We rise and tip the desert from our shoes, reaching for jackets.
Even here it can grow chilly after nightfall.

Khephren – Fourth Dynasty

Impossible in this heat and awful hush
not to imagine him
plotting his progress through eternity,
gathering his slaves, his jewels, his cooking pots,
taking precautions,
posting his monstrous guard.

Impossible not to wonder if he feared,
just for a moment
among his temples and magnificence,
(watching the desert shift and settle
under its load of dynasties and sand),
that this was all.

There is so much dying here,
such thirst and burning
when the wind comes down from Libya, worrying the dust,
the dunes that shimmer nourishing no life,
sustaining only the dark gape of tombs,
the huge sarcophagi prised from skinflint rock.

Unwind the bandages. Dead Pharaoh shrivels to a doll,
his papery skin closes on vacancy,
cloth plugs the hollows where his mind ran out.
The sun has finished with him. He belongs to shadow.
Impossible not to wonder how he fared,
or if he fared at all on that long voyage.

The bright stone remains.
More durable than bone, stronger than sinew
his monuments usurp his silent tongue,
mouth his defiance of mortality.
Impossible in face of these to doubt
he drove beyond dearth and darkness to the light.

In Search of Homer

How many Troys at Hissarlik?
How many layers of stone and legend,
mores and monuments under the rubble
and the restless wind? And which is Ilium?
A few gold beads, a loom abandoned, a skull,
a shattered oil-jar. Every century or so
catastrophe while the gods turn a deaf ear
and generations slide over the edge of memory.

A tremor. Earth opens but the soil runs back.
Annihilation, but more years, more incidents
rush in, plugging the hole in history
too fast for us to hear Cassandra's scream
while the black Mycenaean ships
turn at Tenedos and the carved engine snarls
above Priam's turrets, ghastly in torchlight,
its belly swollen with another dying.

At Pompeii

Noon and the sun concedes no shadow.
Only the beaded lizard,
hot belly on hot stone,
flashed and is gone.

History winks at me round corners.
The guide knows his place, steamy and portentous
with his retinue of exhausted cotton dresses.
His voice dies among cypresses.

Earth here is a hungry mother,
returning grass and thistles with empty hands.
Bone and blood have not worked their purpose
with the soil. They are indurate, petrified.

The stones cannot bear the silence.
They tap at my feet impatiently,
pay heed, pay heed. They would like me
to walk devoutly, a veil over my head.

If I let my attention wander
they will raise temples around me, diminish me
with columns, like the people who built here
under the mountain's frown, until the morning

when the deep thunder tore them from sleep
and the grey falling rain
cancelled the screams on their stretched mouths
and shuttered their incredulous eyes.

Overhead the sky crouches,
waiting for the next incident.

IV

Transplant

The theatre is silent as held breath.
Moments fall and settle gently
on the white table where the patient
sleeps his arctic winter; the flesh
pinned back like a housewife's hem
exposing the intricate red needlework,
torn finery which I must patch and cobble.

Everything is ready. The anaesthetist
roosts in his thicket of tubes.
Glass dials look up at him. Anxiously
he studies their expressions.
I stand apart, visored and antiseptic,
with my steel dishes and scalpels
and gobbets of cotton wool.

The heart goes in with no trouble at all.

But I am not God, though acolytes
white-sheeted leap to my command
and my hands glisten with miracles.
What if I seal despair into this hollow
or stitch an alien grief to these red strings?
Come, these are not the Middle Ages. I must
forget such things. Blood cannot think,
gristle and sinew have no memory.

The valves open and shut satisfactorily.
They have not forgotten.

Waiting

Your bed is by the window. All day
a tree raps at the panes with twisted knuckles,
a tree-coloured bird brooding on one branch.

Metal clangs, reverberates – pipes, troubled
and intestinal, trolleys, cot-sides, hollow
canisters. Above their clatter I cannot

hear your urgent conversation with your pillow.
'Nil by Mouth.' Over your head a placard
hangs lop-sided and at your feet

a map of you, a thin line plotting your
peaks and troughs. Other beds are open
books publishing names and particulars –

damaged children, the sick joke of senility,
women in faded bedroom colours who drag
the luggage of their wounds,

and the patient opposite back from surgery,
bandaged like a parcel, clumsily-wrapped.
Around her they close the curtains. The doctor

hurries with his acolytes and a smell of ether
while visitors pass by in colours gaudy as health.
Tomorrow the tree will rap monotonously

at your window. The birds will print
their angular shorthand on the sky,
the pipes relay their anxious messages.

But the visitors, with flowers and oranges
will pass you by, on tiptoe.
Tomorrow they will close your curtains.

The Ailing Aunts

There were three of them, making it easier
for us to mock. The Three Weird Sisters,
we called them, or the Greek Chorus,
something at any rate dire and sonorous.

They were always checking each other's pulses,
ransacking cupboards for a thermometer,
disappearing under towels in a frenzy of Friar's
Balsam, or doing breathing exercises noisily.

They had hearts, arthritis, sensitive digestions
and various non-specific allergies
and they dined out on their 'ops' for years,
for ill-health was something to be cultivated,

providing it was neither wet nor smelly. It
suggested constitutional fragility like rare
porcelain. (Health was rude, opened its bowels
with clockwork regularity and sweated after exercise.)

They wouldn't make old bones, they said, hadn't
the stamina. There were references to terminal
conditions. They envisaged dying heroically, hands
limp, complexion fever-bright against starched linen.

In the end they never had to cope with cancer
or colostomy, or learn that illness could be
messy, needing its dressings changed.
They were lucky, I suppose, spent their last

days in geriatric wards where appearances didn't
matter and they developed enormous appetites,
wore awful dresses from a common pool
and wet their knickers when they felt like it,

and there were no deathbed leavetakings.
They died undramatically, too far gone
to exploit the possibilities,
wasting the opportunity of a lifetime.

Geriatric Ward

Click click click
        go
          the bars of her cot.

The metal orchestrates her furious tussle
with the restraining sheets, her lower jaw
flopping helplessly like a grounded fish.
Unformed syllables, droplets of saliva fall
from the soft toothless circle of her mouth.

She arrived in the night, out of nothing,
like a new species, a postscript to creation.
It was not like this before. I had learned to accept
our half-world, the amorphous hummocks under
the bedclothes, the gnarled inert fingers,
pink pates gleaming through thin hair,
the rattle of tooth-mugs, orisons in the grey dawn.

But now her frenzied swivel eye seeks mine
continually. I must enclose myself
in my little cretonne kingdom. Her dementia
like a virus may leap the empty space between
her skull and mine and I shall crouch like her,
fighting the swaddle of hospital blankets.

Click click click
        will go
          the bars of my cot.

Room Service

We have no stretcher cases here, nor sirens shrieking
emergency and blood. Infirmity arrives sedately
wearing no bandages for the bleeding stopped
long ago. Now there is only scar-tissue, the site
of ancient battle-grounds whose origins no one remembers.
There are no

visible fractures and we have not the technology to mend
the cracks that widen between reality and dream.
Sometimes we are your children, given boiled sweets,
asked questions which we have no time to answer;
sometimes your mothers: you are pettish, querulous,
needing love

and we offer you bedsocks and barley water, air cushions,
laxatives and Benger's Food. We rub backs and tauten
draw-sheets, empty commodes and fill hot water bottles,
check temperature and pulse. Linen snaps and crackles
on the line; junket cools on larger shelves;
our world revolves

to the rhythm of your hot-house rooms, the chronology
of senescence – a twilit world, crepuscular, as though
the time were always evening, the season perpetual November.
See how our shadows slide before us down long
corridors where carpet digests our footsteps. Listen
at half-open doors

to the conversation of curtain rings, the gas-fire
whispering. Here is your supper-tray. Let us rally
recalcitrant pillows, light lamps, turn the flame higher,
keeping back the dark. That is what we are good at, though
we know, as you in your brief moments of clarity know also,
that we are

all guilty, we are all partners in a grand conspiracy
of silence, for the small hours are hurrying towards us
when currents run sluggish and the pulse ebbs. That is polar
night out there that pushes at the windows. It is quite
star-proof. It will exhaust our feeble candle-power. But
not to-night – not yet.

The Funeral

She knows all the answers now,
he said standing there,
his cassock full of the March gale,
his hands relaxed now, empty of blessings.

Our feet were awkward, the yellowish clay
soiling their respectful polish.
The expensive, out of season flowers
displayed themselves, inviting attention.

Rain was falling. The disordered grave
looked like an unmade bed in that
stone dormitory. At home grief waited
with the sherry glasses, the precise ham sandwiches.

She knows all the answers now
and these we know, rain on the turned earth,
the gulls' cry dying on the wind,
the terrible silence.

Lazarus Rising

This body does not fit well
and the cut is hopelessly obsolete.
Where I come from they wouldn't be seen dead
wearing it; you couldn't give it away.
In fact you'd have to pay them
to take it off your hands.

I didn't think you could get these any more.
It must have come out of the ark
and we all know that lot had no *savoir-faire*.
That time they went to Ararat they were
going to take just what they stood up in,
only God said, take two of everything in case of accidents.

I never liked the material, though I'll admit
it was popular when it first came out.
It's all right when it's new but it doesn't stand up
to hard wear and this one's seen better days.
Besides, it's so coarse and hairy! Feel it.
Can you imagine wearing that next to your soul?

The workmanship is so shoddy. Those seams
won't last five minutes. That's mass production for you.
One leg is obviously shorter than the other
and look at that sort of hump up by the shoulder!
They've forgotten the hair too and I'm sure
there's less than the usual number of teeth.

I'll do anything for you, Lord, you know that.
If my presence helps your cause, then I'm glad I came.
I'll even cram myself into that terrible crumbling body
and make its mouth smile and pretend I'm pleased to be back.
But when it's all over, the miracle and amazement,
the oohs and aahs and the glory to God,

don't fly off to heaven and forget all about me,
trapped in this clumsy jacket of flesh,
remembering its memories. I couldn't bear it –
sickness and worry and being afraid of death,
all that hassle just to survive.
Once is enough to live.

Mother's Room

Right to the end you never got it straight,
the sturdy furniture that knocked
the corners off my childhood. Surfaces powdered
white like the evidence of your slapdash pastry,
drawers never closed and contents on the boil.
Clothes everywhere, the fur, the one good suit
jostling the crêpe and whalebone shabby tackle
rigging your old carcase.

The chimney, stuffed against the draught, now and again
gave birth to a crumpled portion of *The Guardian*.
The mirror faced the wall and never saw
your quick blind dab at the mouth with lipstick
('Do I look all right?'), ramming your strange hats
over disordered hair – unnaturally blackened
product of your wardrobe pharmacy,
the single blow you struck against the years.

Curtains, like you, were always on the move
jangling their rings, tugged furiously
across the glass, in case the man next door
mowing his lawn, or the plumber looking at drains
might see more of yourself than you cared to publish.
Oh it was all storm, it was whirlwind!
Never a day to spare for putting your house
to rights, for sitting back.

Where are you now
with your lambswool socks and toffee wrappers,
your photos on the wall?
Somebody else's taste papers the marks you made
but cannot rub you out, your curtains
hanging silently like records never played,
but every ridge and channel loaded still
with the commotion of your being.